UPDOG

WORLD'S GROSSEST

WORLD'S GROSSEST JOBS

Scott Nickel

Lerner Publications ◆ Minneapolis

Lerner Publications Company
An imprint of Lerner Publishing Group, Inc.
241 First Avenue North
Minneapolis, MN 55401 USA

For reading levels and more information, look up this title at www.lernerbooks.com.

Main body text set in ITC Franklin Gothic Std.
Typeface provided by Adobe Systems.

Designer: Mary Ross
Lerner team: Sue Marquis

Library of Congress Cataloging-in-Publication Data

Names: Nickel, Scott, author.
Title: World's grossest jobs / Scott Nickel.
Description: Minneapolis : Lerner Publications, [2022] | Includes bibliographical references and index. | Audience: Ages 8–11 | Audience: Grades K–1 | Summary: "Get to work on the world's most disgusting jobs. Readers get a close look at these repulsive professions with photos of sewer inspectors and maggot farmers hard at work"—Provided by publisher.
Identifiers: LCCN 2020010238 (print) | LCCN 2020010239 (ebook) | ISBN 9781728403977 (library binding) | ISBN 9781728418971 (ebook)
Subjects: LCSH: Occupations—Juvenile literature. | Vocational guidance—Juvenile literature.
Classification: LCC HF5381.2 .N53 2021 (print) | LCC HF5381.2 (ebook) | DDC 331.702—dc23

LC record available at https://lccn.loc.gov/2020010238
LC ebook record available at https://lccn.loc.gov/2020010239

Manufactured in the United States of America
1-48455-48969-5/26/2021

TABLE OF CONTENTS

DIRTY WORK

From cleaning portable toilets to removing roadkill, some jobs are downright disgusting.

Landfill workers sort through garbage, from rotten food to dirty diapers.

Sewer inspectors spend their days in dirty, smelly water.

Portable toilet cleaners suck up poop and pee.

CREEPY CAREERS

Pest control workers clear infestations of rats.

INFESTATION: to have a large number of

Worm ranchers raise worms to make better soil.

WHICH IS **GROSSER?**

Vomit Collector vs. Leech Collector

Ancient Romans vomited into bowls that vomit collectors picked up.

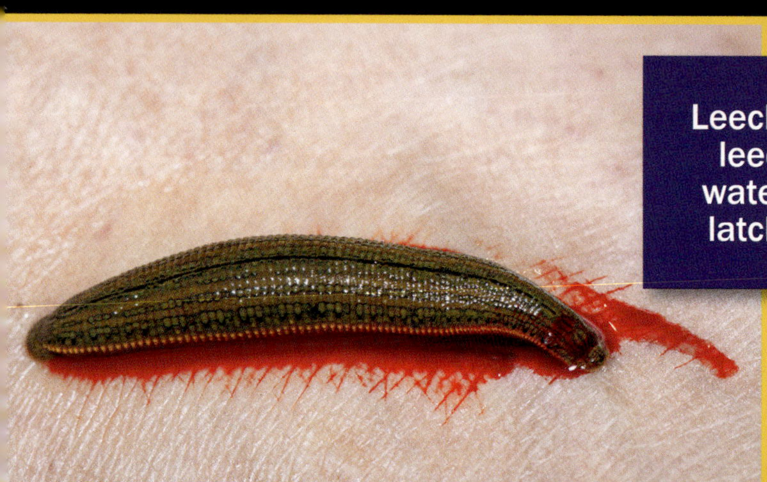

Leech collectors collected leeches by standing in water until the creatures latched on to their skin.

Pet food tasters dine on dog and cat food.

DISGUSTING DIAGRAM!

Maggot farmers raise maggots on rotting food. The farmers sell maggots for fish bait and animal feed.

rotting food
maggot

Bat guano collectors gather bat poop.

GUANO:
waste from birds or bats

Snake milkers squeeze venom out of snakes' mouths to make medicine.

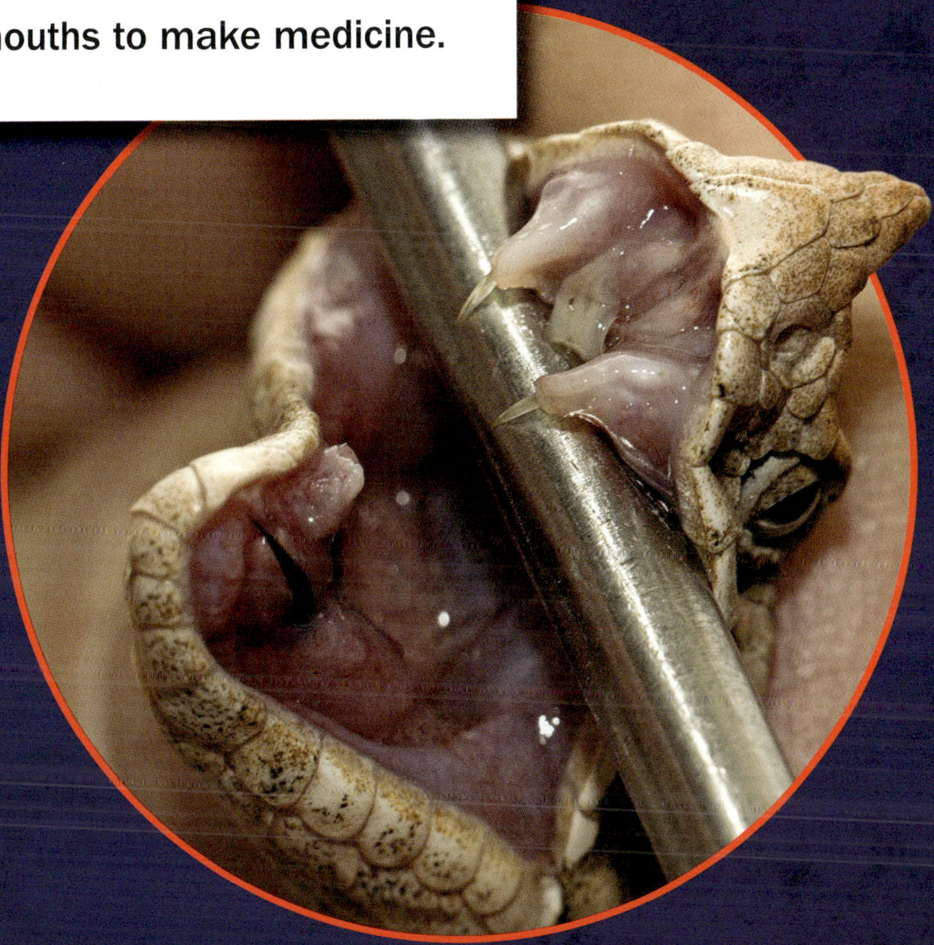

UP NEXT!

DEATH AND DECAY.

DEAD-END JOBS

Crime scene cleaners mop up blood.

Taxidermists stuff dead animals.

Butchers cut up dead chickens, cows, and pigs.

Roadkill collectors scrape dead animals off streets.

Forensic entomologists study bugs in dead people to figure out when they died.

ENTOMOLOGIST: a person who studies insects

FORENSIC: relating to using science to solve crimes

At a crime scene, a blood spatter analyst looks at blood to determine what happened.

These are dirty and gross jobs, but people love doing them.

Glossary

entomologist: a person who studies insects

forensic: relating to using science to solve crimes

guano: waste from birds or bats

infestation: to have a large number of

Check It Out!

Career One Stop: Career Videos
https://www.careeronestop.org/Videos/CareerVideos/career-videos.aspx?lang=en&frd=true

Fort Myers (FL) News-Press: Pet Food Tasters
https://www.news-press.com/story/news/local/2015/11/12/pet-food-taster/75650738/

Kiddle: Leech Facts for Kids
https://kids.kiddle.co/Leech

Nickel, Scott. *World's Grossest Creepy Crawlers.* Minneapolis: Lerner Publications, 2022.

Nickel, Scott. *World's Grossest Human Body Facts.* Minneapolis: Lerner Publications, 2022.

Robinson, Tony. *The Worst Children's Jobs in History.* Sydney: Pan Macmillan, 2017.

Index

Photo Acknowledgments

Image credits: William Hager/Shutterstock.com, p. 4; Perutskyi Petro/Shutterstock.com, p. 5; Vladimir Mulder/Shutterstock.com, p. 6; Peter Gudella/Shutterstock.com, p. 7; M Rose/Shutterstock.com, p. 8; Pixel-Shot/Shutterstock.com, p. 9; Simone Hogan/Shutterstock.com, p. 10 (top); frank60/Shutterstock.com, p. 10 (bottom); Jiri Hera/Shutterstock.com, p. 11; 7th Son Studio/Shutterstock.com, p. 13; Maris Grunskis/Shutterstock.com, p. 14; DEA/C.P. RICCI/Getty Images, p. 15; Photographee.eu/Shutterstock.com, pp. 16, 21; Gregory Stein/Shutterstock.com, p. 17; Salov Evgeniy/Shutterstock.com, p. 18; Panga Media/Shutterstock.com, p. 19; KirinIsHappy/Shutterstock.com, p. 20. Design elements: Saravudh Sudkhaw/Shutterstock.com; Green angel/Shutterstock.com.

Cover: bokan/Shutterstock.com.